The TRAIN YOUR BRAIN

MIND GAMES

156 PUZZLES FOR A SUPERIOR MIND

PETER DE SCHEPPER AND FRANK COUSSEMENT

imagine!

An Imagine Book
Published by Charlesbridge
9 Galen Street
Watertown, MA 02472
617-926-0329
www.imaginebooks.net

Printed in China
10 9 8 7 6 5 4 3 2

ISBN 978-1-62354-087-6

**Do brainteasers or computer games have
a positive impact on brain activity?**

The answer is a resounding "yes." For the last fifteen years we have known that the brain is elastic and it remains so until late in life. Its structure develops constantly as a reaction to your experiences. The more your brain is stimulated, the better your mental condition will be.

An active brain is a better brain.

Proverbial wisdom says "a healthy mind in a healthy body." So you are in control of at least part of this equation. Tests have shown that physical exertion stimulates neurogenesis: those who exercise make significantly more brain cells, which are also granted a longer life. More brain cells ensure better brainpower and better long-term memory.

Brain sport at its best.

This book offers a huge variety of puzzles that will exercise your brain. The puzzles test logical insight, the ability to concentrate, and memory and knowledge. Puzzle solving will not give you a super brain, but you will learn skills for remembering things better and give certain brain activities an extra boost. If you can't solve certain puzzles, don't look up the answers—just try again later. Finding the solution is much more fun than knowing the solution.

1. Word Search

Word searches are one of the most popular types of puzzles. The object of this puzzle is to find and mark all the hidden words inside the grid. The words may be hidden horizontally, vertically or diagonally, in both directions. The letters that remain unused form a key word when read in reading direction.

Hints:

An efficient method for finding the words is to go through the puzzle per column and look for the first letter of the word. If you find one, then look at the surrounding letters to see if the next letter is there. Do this until you find the whole word. Another useful strategy is to look for words with double letters or letters that are highly noticeable such as Q, X and Z.

2. Sudoku

The classic Sudoku with a 9x9 grid is still the most popular one. These completely irresistible, totally addictive puzzles offer a fun challenge that keeps fans entertained for hours. All of our Sudokus can be solved by using logic and were created using human logarithms. You should never have to guess what figure to use.

3. Anagrams

Rearrange the letters of a word or phrase to produce a new word or phrase, using all the original letters exactly once; for example "give her two" can be rearranged into "overweight". Extra letters are already in the right place.

4. Letter Blocks

Move the letter blocks around to form words on top and below that you can associate with a theme. In some puzzles, on one or two blocks, the letter from the top row has been switched with the letter from the bottom row.

5. Brainteasers

To solve our brainteasers you must think logically. Use one or several strategies such as direction, differences and/or similarities, associations, calculations, order, spatial insight, colors, quantities, and distances. Our brainteasers ensure that all of the brain's capacities are utilized.

6. Golf mazes

Start at the cell with a ball and a number on it. Then draw the shortest route from the ball to the hole, the only square without a number. You can only move along vertical and horizontal lines, but not along diagonals. The figure on each square indicates the number of squares the ball must move in the same direction. You can change directions at each stop.

Hints:
Start at the hole and try to find the cell from where you can reach the hole, and then start from the ball.

7. One Letter Less or More
The word below contains the letters of the word above plus or minus the letter in the middle. One letter is already in the right place.

8. Binairo®

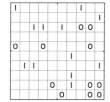

Hey, puzzle fans, get ready for a great new number challenge: Binairo®. These puzzles are just as simple and challenging as Sudoku, but that is where the similarity ends.

Just fill in the grid until there are five zeros and five ones in every row and every column. You can't have more than two of the same number next to or under each other, or have two identical rows or columns.

Hints:
Look for duos of the same number and put the other number before and behind it. Try to avoid trios by entering a zero between two ones or a one between two zeros. Don't

forget to count: if you already have five zeros in a row or column, fill in the rest with ones.

9. Word Pyramid
Each word in the pyramid has the letters of the word above it, plus a new letter.

Hints:
Work your way down from top to bottom. If you can't solve a word, skip the line and try to solve the next one.

10. Doodle puzzle
A doodle puzzle is a combination of images, letters and/or numbers that indicate a word or a concept.

Hints:
If you cannot solve a doodle puzzle, do not look at the answer right away but come back later. Try to think outside the box.

11. Find the Word

Knowing that every arrow points to a letter and that no letter can touch another vertically, horizontally or diagonally, find the missing letters that form a key word when read in order. We show one letter in a circle to help you get started.

Hints:
Cross out all letters that surrounding a letter that you have found.

12. Connect

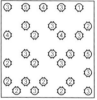 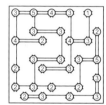

Link all circles with straight horizontal or vertical lines into one connected group. The numbers tell how many lines are connected to a circle. There can be no more than two lines in the same direction and lines cannot cross circles or other lines.

Hints:
A one cannot connect to another one. A two cannot have two connections to another two. A three in a corner must have at least one connection in each direction. A four in a corner has two connections in each direction. A five at the edge must have at least one connection in each direction. A six at the edge has two connections in each direction. A seven in the middle must have at least one connection in each direction. An eight in the middle has two connections in each direction.

So your challenge is to give your brain the best workout it can have, and every one of these puzzles will do that. Enjoy the challenge.

Medium

ALARM
BED
DARK
DECREASE
DEEP
DREAMS
MATTRESS
MORNING
NAP
NEURONS
NIGHT
OBSCURE
REST
RISE
SHEET
SNOOZE
YAWN

S	S	B	S	M	A	E	R	D
D	H	E	Z	O	O	N	S	L
Y	E	D	E	R	B	E	M	N
A	E	E	K	N	S	U	R	I
W	T	R	P	I	C	R	A	G
N	A	S	R	N	U	O	L	H
D	E	N	E	G	R	N	A	T
M	A	T	T	R	E	S	S	P
P	D	E	C	R	E	A	S	E

All the words are hidden vertically, horizontally, or diagonally, in both directions. The letters that remain unused form a key word when read in order.

Easy

						6	8	9	
		1		4			5	
6								
9	7	3	5				1	
8		4	2					5
1	2	8			4	9	3	
	9		1		7	2		
4	3		8	2		5		

*Fill in the grid so that each row, each column,
and each 3x3 frame contains every number from 1 to 9.*

Medium

ENERGY BLAZE (Played Bond in 'On Her Majesty's Secret Servcice')

☐ ☐ **O** ☐ **G** ☐   ☐ ☐ ☐ ☐ ☐ ☐ ☐

FARMHOUSE VISITOR (Bond film with Sean Connery)

☐ ☐ ☐ ☐ ☐ ☐ ☐ ☐ ☐ **W** ☐ ☐ ☐ **L** ☐ ☐ ☐

Form the word or phrase that is described in parentheses with the letters above the grid. Extra letters are already in the right place.

Easy

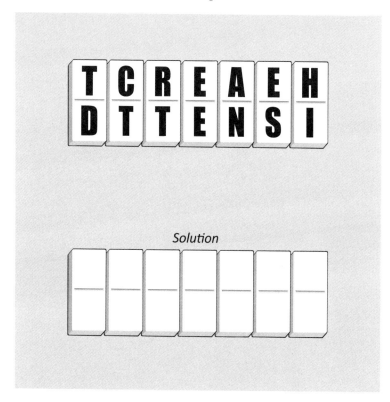

Solution

Move the letter blocks around to form words on top and
below that you can associate with **occupations**.

Hard

The outline is the wrong color for which letter?

Medium

3	4	1	5	1	4
1	2	●	③	0	1
2	3	0	3	4	1
5	1	1	3	1	2
1	4	1	4	1	5
3	5	5	2	4	2

Draw the shortest path from the ball to the hole. You can only move along vertical and horizontal lines. The figure on each square indicates the number of squares the ball must move in the same direction. You can change direction at each stop.

Hard

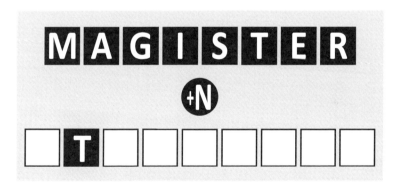

The word below contains the letters of the word above plus or minus the letter in the middle. One letter is already in the right place.

Medium

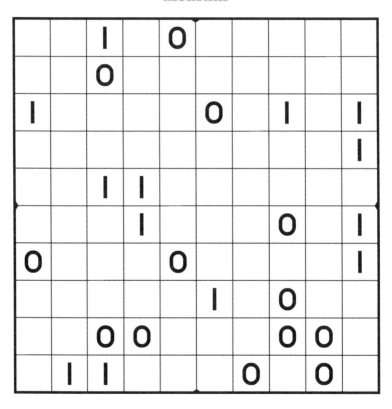

Complete the grid with zeros and ones until there are five zeros and five ones in every row and every column. No more than two of the same number can be next to or under each other. Rows or columns with exactly the same content are not allowed.

Medium

(1) before noon

(2) a sudden very loud noise

(3) glow

(4) assign responsibility

(5) ball of glass

(6) pedestrian

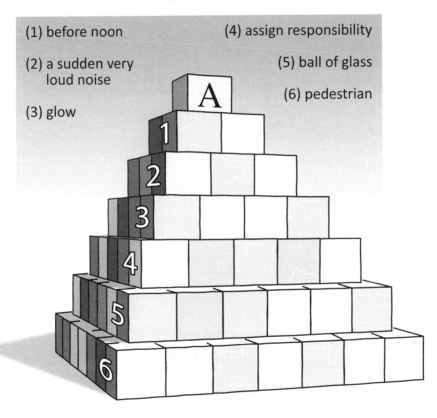

Each word in the pyramid has the letters of the word above it, plus a new letter.

Medium

*What word or concept
is depicted here?*

Easy

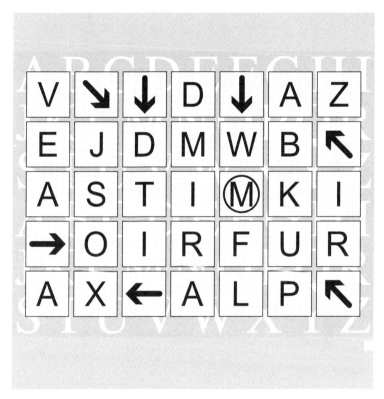

V	↘	↓	D	↓	A	Z
E	J	D	M	W	B	↖
A	S	T	I	Ⓜ	K	I
→	O	I	R	F	U	R
A	X	←	A	L	P	↖

Knowing that every arrow points to a letter and that no letter can touch another vertically, horizontally, or diagonally, find the missing letters that form a key word when read in order. We show one letter in a circle to help you get started.

Very Hard

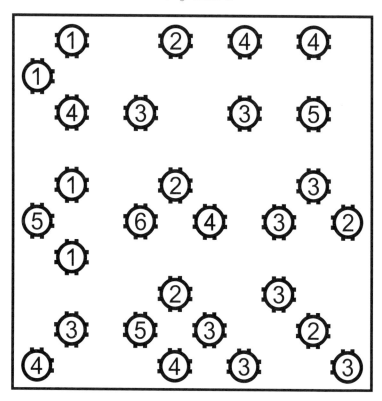

Link all circles with straight horizontal or vertical lines into one connected group. The numbers tell how many lines are connected to a circle. There can be no more than two lines in the same direction and lines cannot cross circles or other lines.

Medium

AIRBUS
ANTONOV
BOMBS
DOUGLAS
FOKKER
FUEL
GLIDE
LAND
NOSE
PASSENGER
PILOT
TAIL
TUPOLEV
WING

A	V	O	N	O	T	N	A	I
G	D	S	P	I	L	O	T	R
L	N	B	G	L	E	S	S	E
I	A	M	N	I	U	E	U	K
D	L	O	I	A	F	R	B	K
E	P	B	W	T	L	A	R	O
V	E	L	O	P	U	T	I	F
N	E	D	O	U	G	L	A	S
P	A	S	S	E	N	G	E	R

All the words are hidden vertically, horizontally, or diagonally, in both directions. The letters that remain unused form a key word when read in order.

Medium

		3	7	5	9			
6	4							
			4			3		
8	5	1		4			3	
4	9		3		5			8
3			8		7			
2	3	4				5	9	1
						8		6
9								

Fill in the grid so that each row, each column,
and each 3x3 frame contains every number from 1 to 9.

Medium

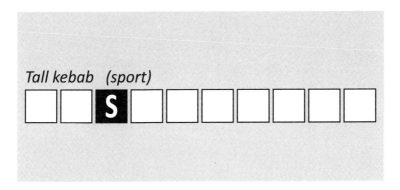

Tall kebab (sport)

| | | S | | | | | | |

OSCARS (Native American sport)

| L | | | | | | | E |

Form the word or phrase that is described in parentheses with the letters above the grid. Extra letters are already in the right place.

Medium

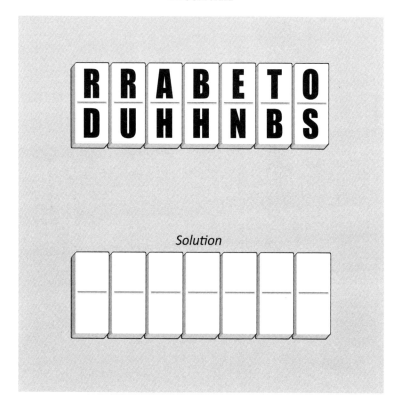

Solution

Move the letter blocks around to form words on top
and below that you can associate with **family**.
The letters are reversed on one block.

Hard

The owners of this modern house are trying to limit energy use to a minimum. Each number stands for the use in a certain room. How much energy will be used in the room with the question mark (the main entrance)?

Medium

1	3	4	4	3	2
5	3	3	1	4	1
1	4	2	1	3	4
2	4	3	0	3	3
3	3	1	1	2	
1	4	5	1	2	1

Draw the shortest path from the ball to the hole. You can only move along vertical and horizontal lines. The figure on each square indicates the number of squares the ball must move in the same direction. You can change direction at each stop.

Hard

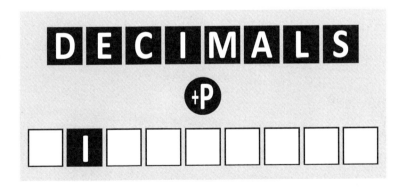

The word below contains the letters of the word above plus or minus the letter in the middle. One letter is already in the right place.

Hard

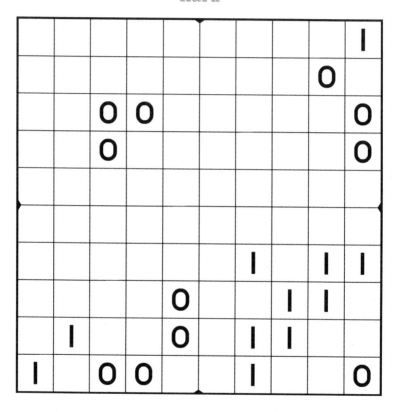

Complete the grid with zeros and ones until there are five zeros
and five ones in every row and every column. No more than two
of the same number can be next to or under each other. Rows
or columns with exactly the same content are not allowed.

Medium

(1) toward the inside

(2) particle

(3) mint

(4) fresh

(5) something done

(6) warn strongly

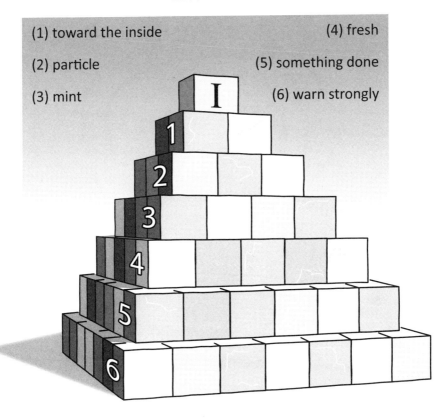

*Each word in the pyramid has the letters of
the word above it, plus a new letter.*

Medium

*What word or concept
is depicted here?*

Medium

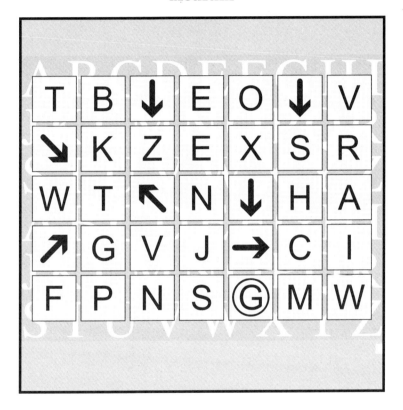

Knowing that every arrow points to a letter and that no letter can touch another vertically, horizontally, or diagonally, find the missing letters that form a key word when read in order. We show one letter in a circle to help you get started.

Medium

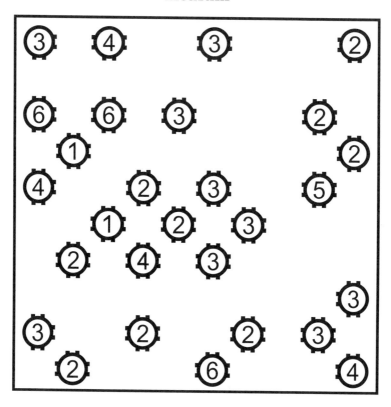

Link all circles with straight horizontal or vertical lines into one connected group. The numbers tell how many lines are connected to a circle. There can be no more than two lines in the same direction and lines cannot cross circles or other lines.

Medium

ACTOR
ALIBI
ASSAULT
BROWN
CHASE
COURT
DARK
JURY
LUDLUM
POLITICS
SCRIPT
SEVEN
STORY
VICTIM
WITNESS

T	P	A	S	S	A	U	L	T
S	T	O	R	Y	D	A	R	K
H	M	U	L	D	U	L	T	R
M	I	T	C	I	V	I	P	N
I	L	J	T	C	T	B	I	E
L	E	R	U	R	H	I	R	V
A	C	T	O	R	U	A	C	E
N	W	O	R	B	Y	O	S	S
S	S	E	N	T	I	W	C	E

All the words are hidden vertically, horizontally,
or diagonally, in both directions. The letters that remain
unused form a key word when read in order.

Hard

		6			2	7		
7		1	4				6	2
	8	9				1		
		3					9	
		7						6
	4			9	8			
					5	9		3
			1		7	8		

*Fill in the grid so that each row, each column,
and each 3x3 frame contains every number from 1 to 9.*

Medium

MOONSTAR *(stargazer)*

			R				E	

MASTER PET *(a diagrammatic representation of a city)*

Form the word or phrase that is described in parentheses with the letters above the grid. Extra letters are already in the right place.

Easy

Solution

*Move the letter blocks around to form words on top and below that you can associate with **American cars**.*

Medium

Each can lists the points you will earn if you throw a snowball into the can.
How many points will you earn for the can with a question mark?

Medium

2	4	1	3	5	5
5	3	3	3	2	5
4	3	1	3	2	
5	2	1	0	1	4
1	3	2	4	2	3
4	2	4	3	3	3

Draw the shortest path from the ball to the hole. You can only move along vertical and horizontal lines. The figure on each square indicates the number of squares the ball must move in the same direction. You can change direction at each stop.

Hard

The word below contains the letters of the word
above plus or minus the letter in the middle.
One letter is already in the right place.

Easy

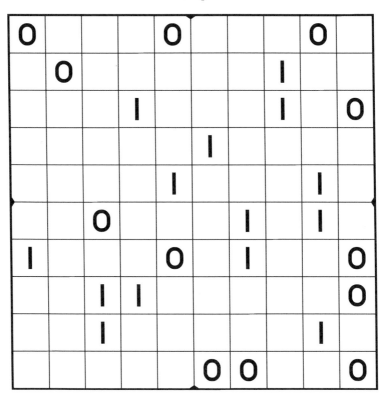

Complete the grid with zeros and ones until there are five zeros and five ones in every row and every column. No more than two of the same number can be next to or under each other. Rows or columns with exactly the same content are not allowed.

WORD PYRAMID

Medium

(1) change location

(2) inflated feeling of pride

(3) 45th Vice President of the U.S.

(4) makeup

(5) mortuary

(6) gastronome

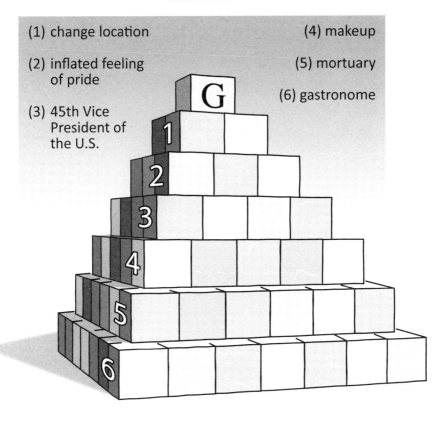

Each word in the pyramid has the letters of the word above it, plus a new letter.

Medium

*What word or concept
is depicted here?*

Hard

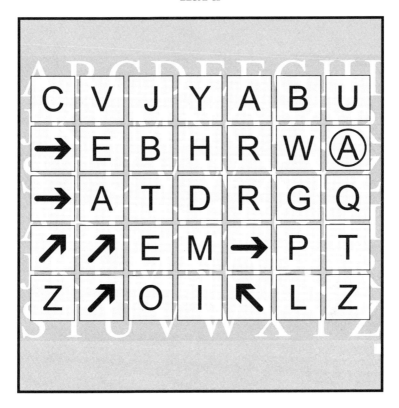

Knowing that every arrow points to a letter and that no letter can touch another vertically, horizontally, or diagonally, find the missing letters that form a key word when read in order. We show one letter in a circle to help you get started.

Easy

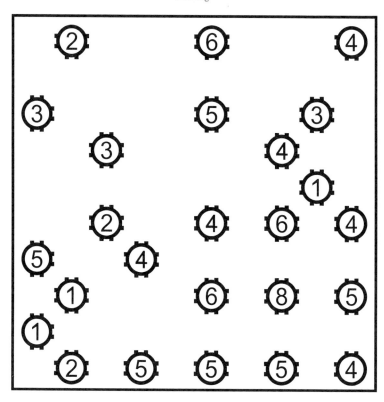

Link all circles with straight horizontal or vertical lines into one connected group. The numbers tell how many lines are connected to a circle. There can be no more than two lines in the same direction and lines cannot cross circles or other lines.

Medium

BISHOP
BLOCK
CHAMPION
DRAW
ENDGAME
GAMBIT
KING
KNIGHT
MASTER
MINIATURE
PAWN
RESIGN
ROOK
WING
WINNER

E	R	U	T	A	I	N	I	M
D	R	A	W	R	O	O	K	E
C	E	I	R	E	S	I	G	N
H	N	K	E	P	G	B	T	D
G	N	I	T	A	A	I	H	G
E	I	N	S	W	M	S	G	A
S	W	G	A	N	B	H	I	M
C	H	A	M	P	I	O	N	E
B	L	O	C	K	T	P	K	S

*All the words are hidden vertically, horizontally,
or diagonally, in both directions. The letters that remain
unused form a key word when read in order.*

Easy

3	4	1		9	6	8	2	5
	8		3			1	7	
			2		8	6	4	3
			6	3				8
	3			7	2	4		1
		8			1			
	2							7
	1			6				
9								

*Fill in the grid so that each row, each column,
and each 3x3 frame contains every number from 1 to 9.*

Medium

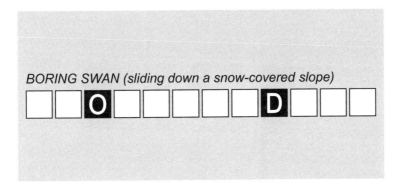

BORING SWAN *(sliding down a snow-covered slope)*

☐ ☐ **O** ☐ ☐ ☐ ☐ **D** ☐ ☐ ☐

JUNE BUG *(it will get you suspended)*

☐ ☐ ☐ ☐ ☐ **E** ☐ ☐ **M** **P**

Form the word or phrase that is described in parentheses with the letters above the grid. Extra letters are already in the right place.

Medium

Solution

Move the letter blocks around to form words on top and
below that you can associate with **court of justice**.
The letters are reversed on one block.

Medium

Tars & An

Peter & Eve

Daren & Edna

Said & Sita

Ryan ?

Elsie

Mary

Annie

Carey

Who (Elsie, Mary, Annie or Carey) is Ryan's girlfriend?

GOLF MAZE

Medium

3	2	5	5	3	1
4	1	2	2	4	1
4	4	2	2	4	5
2	0	1	3	1	1
4	1	4	4	2	4
4		5	3	1	3

Draw the shortest path from the ball to the hole. You can only move along vertical and horizontal lines. The figure on each square indicates the number of squares the ball must move in the same direction. You can change direction at each stop.

Hard

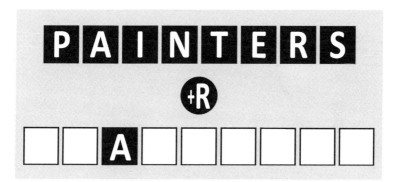

*The word below contains the letters of the word
above plus or minus the letter in the middle.
One letter is already in the right place.*

Very Hard

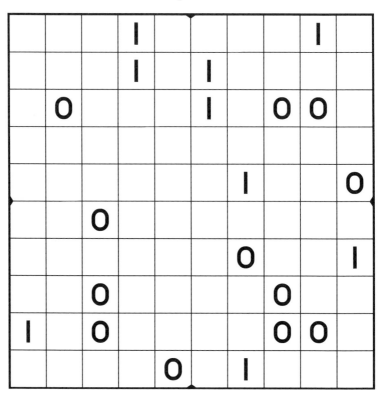

Complete the grid with zeros and ones until there are five zeros and five ones in every row and every column. No more than two of the same number can be next to or under each other. Rows or columns with exactly the same content are not allowed.

Medium

(1) I

(2) American rock band

(3) to a greater extent

(4) subway

(5) female parent

(6) vacuum flask

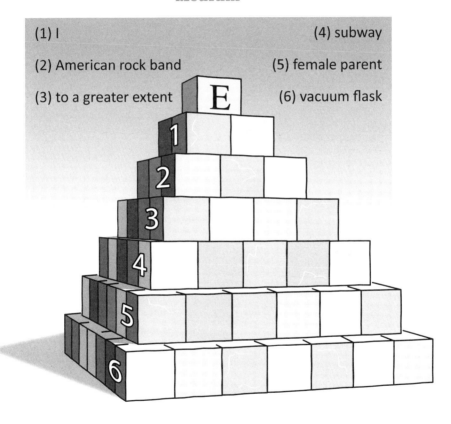

*Each word in the pyramid has the letters of
the word above it, plus a new letter.*

Medium

What word or concept is depicted here?

FIND THE WORD

Easy

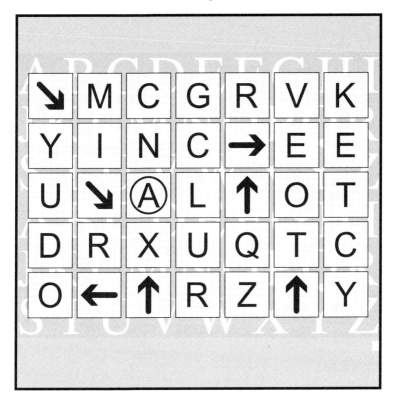

*Knowing that every arrow points to a letter and that no letter
can touch another vertically, horizontally, or diagonally, find
the missing letters that form a key word when read in order.
We show one letter in a circle to help you get started.*

Hard

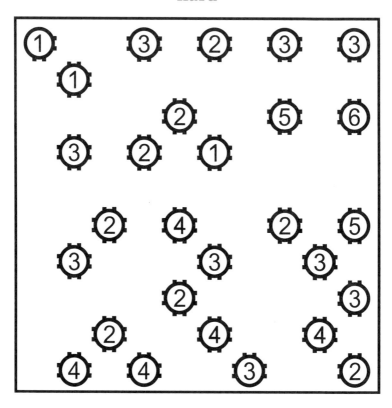

Link all circles with straight horizontal or vertical lines into one connected group. The numbers tell how many lines are connected to a circle. There can be no more than two lines in the same direction and lines cannot cross circles or other lines.

Medium

AFRICA
BAKER
BEBOP
BLUES
EVANS
IMPULSE
MILES
MONK
PIANO
REINHARDT
SLAVES
SOLO
TRUMPET
TUBA
VOODOO

```
R A B B E B O P J
E B A A B L U E S
I U K V O O D O O
N T E S E V A L S
H T R U M P E T E
A K P I A N O Z L
R N A C I R F A I
D O Z E V A N S M
T M I M P U L S E
```

*All the words are hidden vertically, horizontally,
or diagonally, in both directions. The letters that remain
unused form a key word when read in order.*

Medium

							7	
3		2					6	
		4		6		8		
		5			8			
	7						5	
	9				1		4	6
	2		1				9	3
9				4		1	8	5
	8		5	9	3			7

Fill in the grid so that each row, each column,
and each 3x3 frame contains every number from 1 to 9.

Medium

A BARN (Cornhusker State)

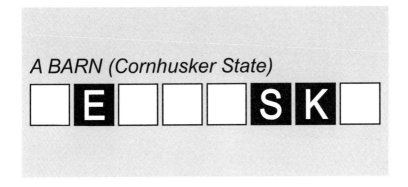

	E				S	K	

EX WOMEN (Land of Enchantment)

| | | | | | | | I | C | |

Form the word or phrase that is described in parentheses with the letters above the grid. Extra letters are already in the right place.

Hard

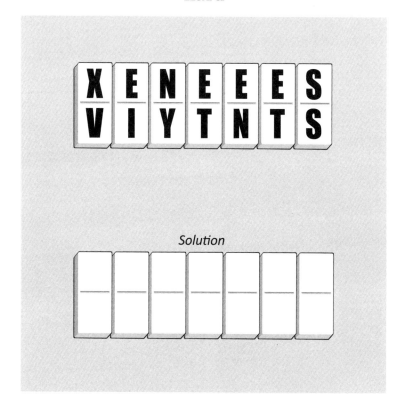

Solution

Move the letter blocks around to form words on top
and below that you can associate with **numbers**.
The letters are reversed on two blocks.

Hard

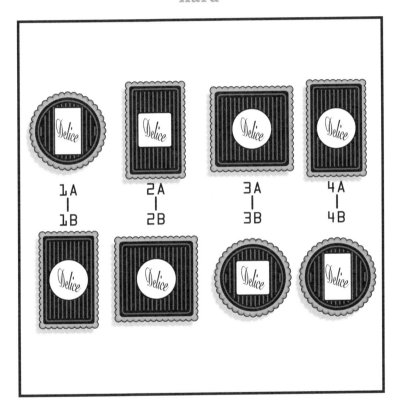

Which group of biscuits (1-4) does not belong?

Medium

3	2	4	5	4	3
1	2	1	3	1	1
3	1	2	3	4	5
1	0	1	1	2	3
5	4	2	3	4	5
1	2		4	2	0

Draw the shortest path from the ball to the hole. You can only move along vertical and horizontal lines. The figure on each square indicates the number of squares the ball must move in the same direction. You can change direction at each stop.

Hard

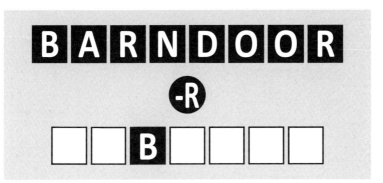

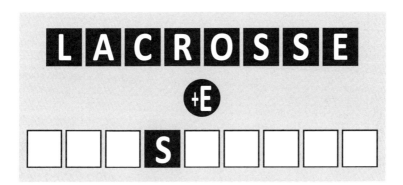

The word below contains the letters of the word above plus or minus the letter in the middle. One letter is already in the right place.

Medium

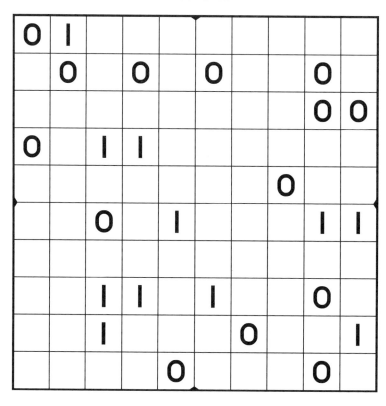

Complete the grid with zeros and ones until there are five zeros
and five ones in every row and every column. No more than two
of the same number can be next to or under each other. Rows
or columns with exactly the same content are not allowed.

Medium

(1) used before a vowel

(2) insect living in organized colonies

(3) military alliance

(4) dance

(5) candy

(6) frequently visited place

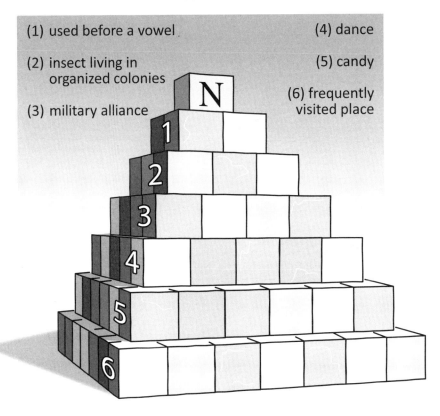

Each word in the pyramid has the letters of the word above it, plus a new letter.

Medium

*What word or concept
is depicted here?*

Medium

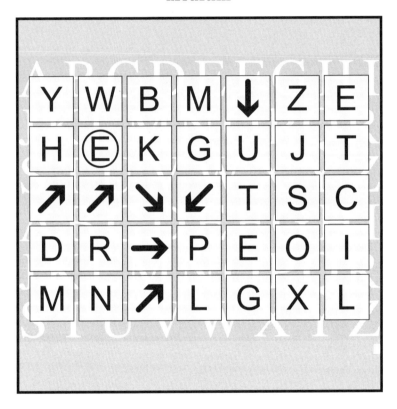

Knowing that every arrow points to a letter and that no letter can touch another vertically, horizontally, or diagonally, find the missing letters that form a key word when read in order. We show one letter in a circle to help you get started.

Medium

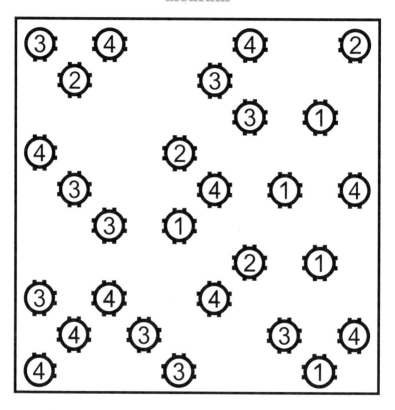

Link all circles with straight horizontal or vertical lines into
one connected group. The numbers tell how many lines are
connected to a circle. There can be no more than two lines in
the same direction and lines cannot cross circles or other lines.

Medium

ABSEIL

BALANCE

BRIDGING

FLAG

GRIP

HARNESS

INDOOR

KNOTS

LEG LOOP

MAGNESIUM

ROCK

ROPE

SCORE

SCREW

M	A	G	N	E	S	I	U	M
B	S	S	A	E	K	N	S	P
R	S	C	R	C	S	D	T	O
I	E	O	O	N	C	O	O	O
D	N	R	P	A	R	O	N	L
G	R	E	E	L	E	R	K	G
I	A	L	P	A	W	I	N	E
N	H	L	A	B	S	E	I	L
G	I	S	F	G	R	I	P	M

All the words are hidden vertically, horizontally,
or diagonally, in both directions. The letters that remain
unused form a key word when read in order.

Hard

	5	7						
6		3				2		
				2		8		
				6				
	9	5		7	8			
					7	1	8	
		1	9	4			3	
	2			8	6	4	5	

Fill in the grid so that each row, each column,
and each 3x3 frame contains every number from 1 to 9.

Medium

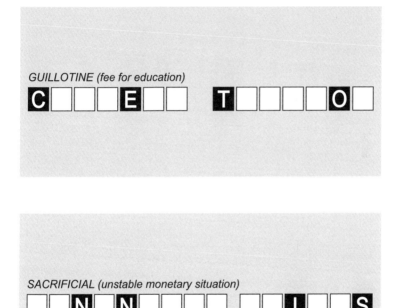

GUILLOTINE (fee for education)

C □ □ □ E □ □   T □ □ □ O □

SACRIFICIAL (unstable monetary situation)

□ □ N □ N □ □ □ □   □ □ I □ □ S

Form the word or phrase that is described in parentheses with the letters above the grid. Extra letters are already in the right place.

Easy

Solution

*Move the letter blocks around to form words on top
and below that you can associate with **athletics**.*

Hard

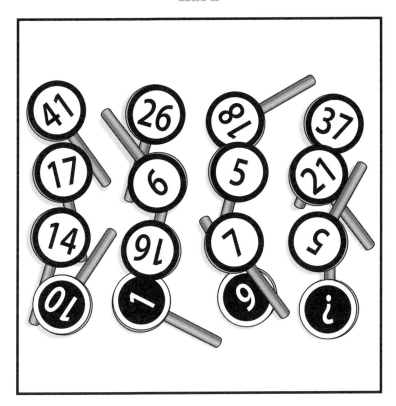

Which number should replace the question mark?

Medium

4	●	5	4	1	4
5	4	1	2	③	5
3	3	1	1	4	3
3	2	1	1	0	5
3	1	4	4	1	1
1	2	4	4	2	4

Draw the shortest path from the ball to the hole. You can only move along vertical and horizontal lines. The figure on each square indicates the number of squares the ball must move in the same direction. You can change direction at each stop.

Hard

*The word below contains the letters of the word
above plus or minus the letter in the middle.
One letter is already in the right place.*

Hard

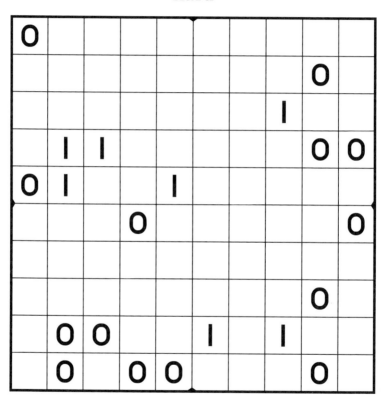

Complete the grid with zeros and ones until there are five zeros and five ones in every row and every column. No more than two of the same number can be next to or under each other. Rows or columns with exactly the same content are not allowed.

Medium

(1) point in time

(2) strike lightly

(3) record

(4) ace

(5) leave

(6) cornered

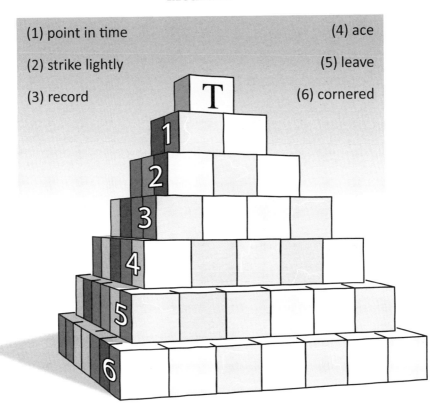

*Each word in the pyramid has the letters of
the word above it, plus a new letter.*

Hard

*What word or concept
is depicted here?*

Hard

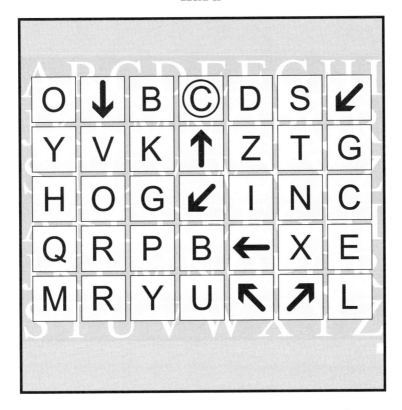

Knowing that every arrow points to a letter and that no letter can touch another vertically, horizontally, or diagonally, find the missing letters that form a key word when read in order. We show one letter in a circle to help you get started.

Easy

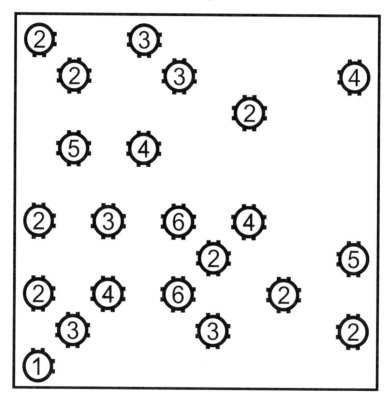

Link all circles with straight horizontal or vertical lines into one connected group. The numbers tell how many lines are connected to a circle. There can be no more than two lines in the same direction and lines cannot cross circles or other lines.

Medium

AISNE
COLORADO
CONGO
DANUBE
ELBE
GANGES
HUDSON
ISONZO
KUBAN
MARNE
MISSOURI
NECKAR
RHINE
TAGUS
THAMES
TIGRIS

```
C R I I S O N Z O
I O E E B U N A D
R H N G A N G E S
U U R G K U B A N
O D A R O L O C T
S S M H E N S I A
S O S I R G I T V
I N E N E C K A R
M R S E M A H T S
```

*All the words are hidden vertically, horizontally,
or diagonally, in both directions. The letters that remain
unused form a key word when read in order.*

Very Hard

		7	4				9	1
3								
	4		1	6	5		7	
	6		7	2				4
5					6			
		9				2		8
			2			4		3
				5				7
						1		

Fill in the grid so that each row, each column,
and each 3x3 frame contains every number from 1 to 9.

Medium

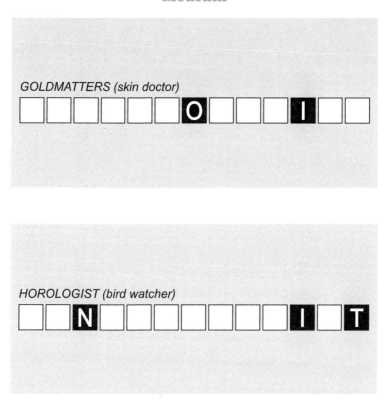

GOLDMATTERS (skin doctor)

| | | | | | | O | | | I | | |

HOROLOGIST (bird watcher)

| | | N | | | | | | | I | | T |

Form the word or phrase that is described in parentheses with the letters above the grid. Extra letters are already in the right place.

Medium

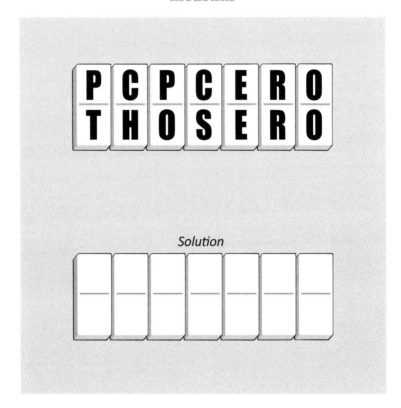

P C P C E R O
T H O S E R O

Solution

---

*Move the letter blocks around to form words on top and
below that you can associate with **motorcycles**.
The letters are reversed on one block.*

Very hard

Which flower branch (1-6) does not belong?

Medium

1	4	5	1	4	4
5	4	1	3	4	3
3	2	3	3	4	2
1	3	1		3	5
2	2	1	4	0	2
3	1	4	3	1	2

Draw the shortest path from the ball to the hole. You can only move along vertical and horizontal lines. The figure on each square indicates the number of squares the ball must move in the same direction. You can change direction at each stop.

Hard

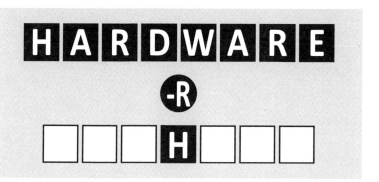

The word below contains the letters of the word above plus or minus the letter in the middle. One letter is already in the right place.

Easy

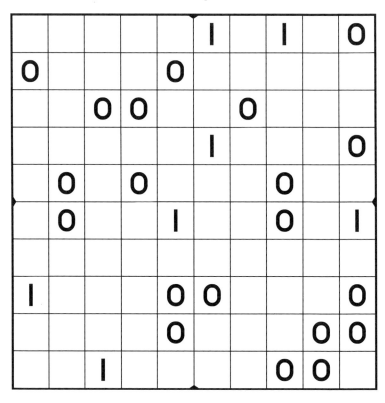

Complete the grid with zeros and ones until there are five zeros and five ones in every row and every column. No more than two of the same number can be next to or under each other. Rows or columns with exactly the same content are not allowed.

Medium

(1) exist

(2) insect

(3) brewski

(4) renegade

(5) pitch range of the highest female voice

(6) shake

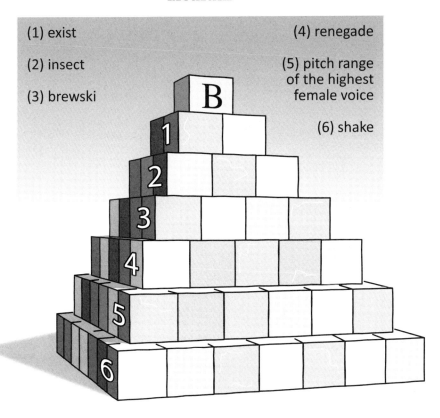

Each word in the pyramid has the letters of the word above it, plus a new letter.

Hard

*What word or concept
is depicted here?*

Easy

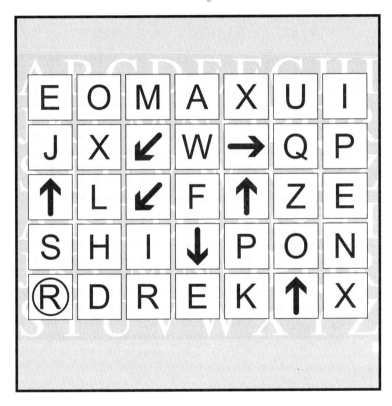

Knowing that every arrow points to a letter and that no letter can touch another vertically, horizontally, or diagonally, find the missing letters that form a key word when read in order. We show one letter in a circle to help you get started.

Very Hard

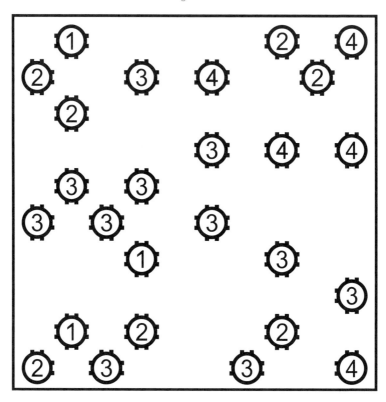

Link all circles with straight horizontal or vertical lines into one connected group. The numbers tell how many lines are connected to a circle. There can be no more than two lines in the same direction and lines cannot cross circles or other lines.

Medium

APRICOT
BANANA
CURRANT
DATE
FIG
GRAPE
GUAVA
LEMON
LIME
MANGO
PAPAYA
PEACH
PITAYA
PLUM
POMELO
QUINCE

```
A A T N A R R U C
V E N P O M E L O
A T E A P E A C H
U A M P N O M E L
G D I A L A F C O
R U L Y I U B N G
P I T A Y A M I N
T G R A P E F U A
A P R I C O T Q M
```

*All the words are hidden vertically, horizontally,
or diagonally, in both directions. The letters that remain
unused form a key word when read in order.*

Easy

			5	6	7			
	1	6	3	9	2		4	
7	5		4		8	3	6	2
	7			8	1		5	6
4			2	7	3			9
9								
				3				
		2				6		1
						7		

*Fill in the grid so that each row, each column,
and each 3x3 frame contains every number from 1 to 9.*

Medium

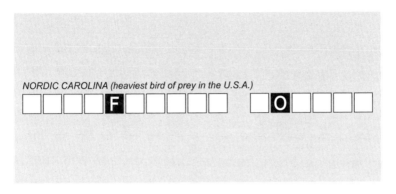

NORDIC CAROLINA (heaviest bird of prey in the U.S.A.)

☐ ☐ ☐ ☐ **F** ☐ ☐ ☐ ☐ ☐   ☐ **O** ☐ ☐ ☐ ☐

CENTRAL HEAP (largest living land mammal)

☐ **F** ☐ **I** ☐ ☐ **N** ☐   ☐ ☐ ☐ ☐ ☐ **A** ☐ ☐

Form the word or phrase that is described in parentheses with the letters above the grid. Extra letters are already in the right place.

Hard

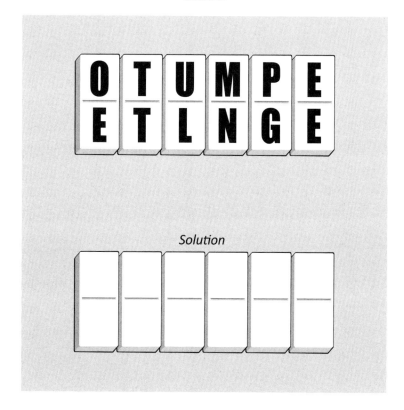

Solution

Move the letter blocks around to form words on top
and below that you can associate with **body parts**.
The letters are reversed on two blocks.

Medium

*What is the name of the sixth person
that will receive a greeting card?*

Medium

2	5	1	4	5	2
2	2	3	3	2	2
2	4	1	2	4	4
2	4	1	2	1	2
1	2	2	2	4	1
4	1		5	1	5

Draw the shortest path from the ball to the hole. You can only move along vertical and horizontal lines. The figure on each square indicates the number of squares the ball must move in the same direction. You can change direction at each stop.

Hard

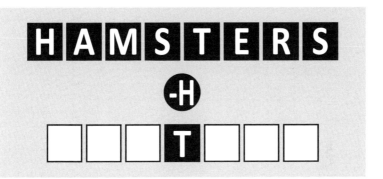

The word below contains the letters of the word
above plus or minus the letter in the middle.
One letter is already in the right place.

Very Hard

0									
	0				1				0
			1	1		0			0
			1	1		0			
		1						0	
			1				0		
	0								
1	0	0				1			1
			0	0		0	0		1

Complete the grid with zeros and ones until there are five zeros and five ones in every row and every column. No more than two of the same number can be next to or under each other. Rows or columns with exactly the same content are not allowed.

Medium

(1) helium

(2) of a female

(3) long-eared mammal

(4) 3rd planet from the sun

(5) source of danger

(6) dramatic art

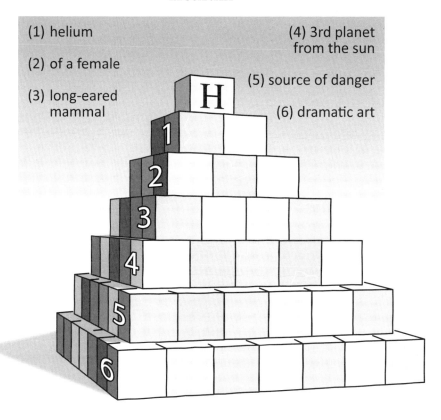

Each word in the pyramid has the letters of the word above it, plus a new letter.

Medium

*What word or concept
is depicted here?*

Medium

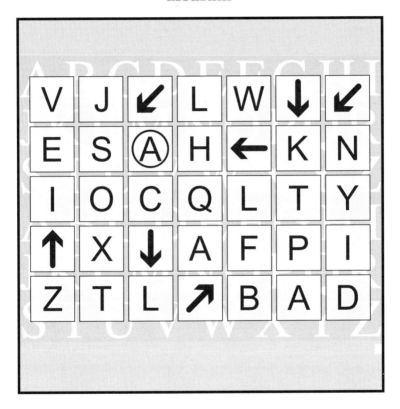

Knowing that every arrow points to a letter and that no letter can touch another vertically, horizontally, or diagonally, find the missing letters that form a key word when read in order. We show one letter in a circle to help you get started.

Hard

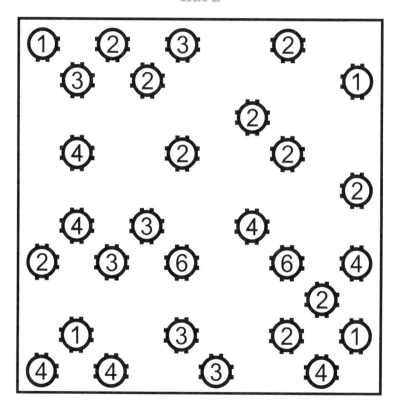

Link all circles with straight horizontal or vertical lines into
one connected group. The numbers tell how many lines are
connected to a circle. There can be no more than two lines in
the same direction and lines cannot cross circles or other lines.

Medium

AIDA

ARIA

BERLIOZ

COMIC

DRAMA

GLUCK

MOZART

NORMA

ORATORIO

OTHELLO

PLAY

RAMEAU

SONG

TENOR

ZARZUELA

```
A O O T H E L L O
L G L U C K A Z R
E A G N O S M O A
U C I M O C A I T
Z P A D E R R L O
R A M E A U D R R
A R R O N E T E I
Z I O Y A L P B O
A A N T R A Z O M
```

*All the words are hidden vertically, horizontally,
or diagonally, in both directions. The letters that remain
unused form a key word when read in order.*

Medium

						2		
	7	6			8			
	8	3				9	7	
			6					
				9			3	
4						8		
		7	4			3		2
1				3			8	4
3	4	2	1	8	6	7	5	

Fill in the grid so that each row, each column,
and each 3x3 frame contains every number from 1 to 9.

Medium

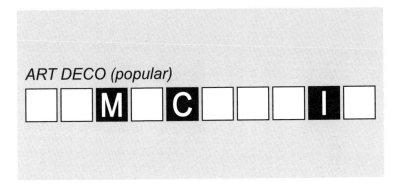

ART DECO (popular)

| | | M | | C | | | | I | |

A PENCIL (in opposition to a monarchy)

| R | | | U | B | | | | |

Form the word or phrase that is described in parentheses with the letters above the grid. Extra letters are already in the right place.

Easy

Solution

Move the letter blocks around to form words on top
and below that you can associate with **dances**.

Hard

Which butterfly (A-D) doesn't belong to the same family?

Medium

3	4	4	5	5	1
2	2	4	2	(3)	2
4	3	3	0	3	2
3	4	2	3	4	5
1	4	4	2	4	2
3	4	5	5	5	⬤

Draw the shortest path from the ball to the hole. You can only move along vertical and horizontal lines. The figure on each square indicates the number of squares the ball must move in the same direction. You can change direction at each stop.

Hard

*The word below contains the letters of the word
above plus or minus the letter in the middle.
One letter is already in the right place.*

Medium

	0	I							
0	I		I		I		I		
						0		0	I
		0	0						
0			0						0
	0	0							
								0	
		I						0	
				I					
					0	0		0	0

Complete the grid with zeros and ones until there are five zeros and five ones in every row and every column. No more than two of the same number can be next to or under each other. Rows or columns with exactly the same content are not allowed.

Medium

(1) negative

(2) immeasurably long period of time

(3) organ

(4) disturbance

(5) older

(6) edition

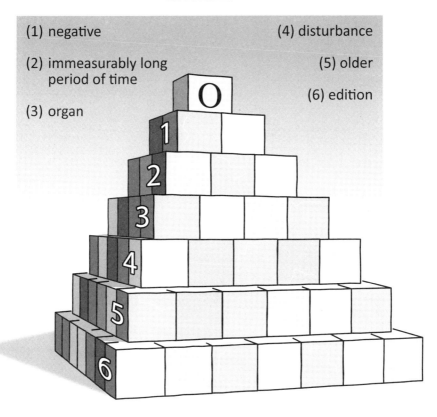

Each word in the pyramid has the letters of the word above it, plus a new letter.

Hard

*What word or concept
is depicted here?*

Hard

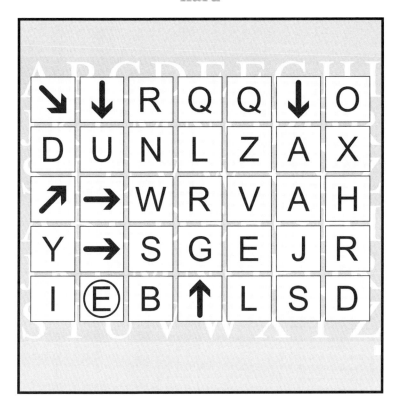

Knowing that every arrow points to a letter and that no letter can touch another vertically, horizontally, or diagonally, find the missing letters that form a key word when read in order. We show one letter in a circle to help you get started.

Medium

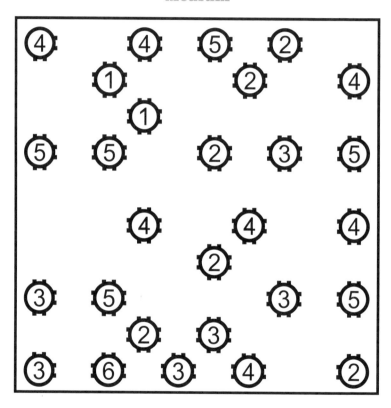

Link all circles with straight horizontal or vertical lines into one connected group. The numbers tell how many lines are connected to a circle. There can be no more than two lines in the same direction and lines cannot cross circles or other lines.

Medium

ARMS
ARTERY
BRAIN
EARS
EYES
GLANDS
HEAD
LIVER
MOLARS
MUSCLES
NAILS
NOSE
SKIN
STOMACH
TISSUE
TONGUE
TORSO

R	Y	B	T	O	N	G	U	E
E	R	O	D	A	E	H	H	D
V	E	U	S	S	I	T	C	M
I	T	M	L	E	T	M	A	U
L	R	I	Y	B	O	S	M	S
A	A	E	R	L	R	K	O	C
N	S	A	A	A	S	I	T	L
Y	I	R	E	S	O	N	S	E
N	S	G	L	A	N	D	S	S

*All the words are hidden vertically, horizontally,
or diagonally, in both directions. The letters that remain
unused form a key word when read in order.*

Hard

	6		3	1				
	4			7	9			8
	1						7	3
		8		5				7
2	7							1
			8					
3			1	6		4		2
						3	6	

Fill in the grid so that each row, each column,
and each 3x3 frame contains every number from 1 to 9.

Medium

HOT WATER *(boundary separating two masses of air)*

☐ **E** ☐ ☐ ☐ **R** ☐ **F** ☐ ☐ **N** ☐

SHORT-TERM *(heavy rain or hail along with thunder and lightning)*

☐ ☐ **U** **N** **D** ☐ ☐ ☐ ☐ ☐ ☐

Form the word or phrase that is described in parentheses with the letters above the grid. Extra letters are already in the right place.

Medium

Solution

*Move the letter blocks around to form words on top
and below that you can associate with **emotions**.
The letters are reversed on one block.*

Medium

*What is the value of the
playing card with the question mark?*

GOLF MAZE

Medium

2	1	1	4	3	2
2	1	1	1	2	2
4	3	2	1	2	2
2	3	1	3	4	3
3	2	2	4	4	1
1	5	1	1		3

Draw the shortest path from the ball to the hole. You can only move along vertical and horizontal lines. The figure on each square indicates the number of squares the ball must move in the same direction. You can change direction at each stop.

Hard

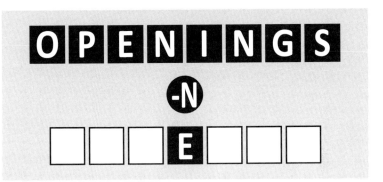

OPENINGS

-N

[ ] [ ] [ ] **E** [ ] [ ] [ ]

PARADISE

+P

[ ] [ ] [ ] [ ] **P** [ ] [ ] [ ] [ ]

The word below contains the letters of the word above plus or minus the letter in the middle. One letter is already in the right place.

Hard

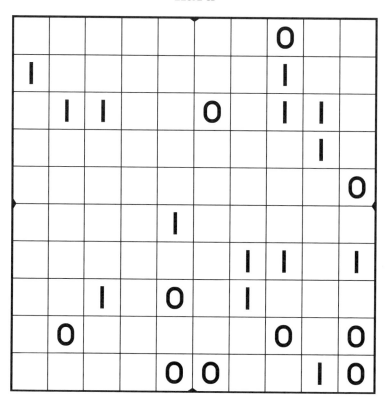

Complete the grid with zeros and ones until there are five zeros and five ones in every row and every column. No more than two of the same number can be next to or under each other. Rows or columns with exactly the same content are not allowed.

Medium

(1) in the direction of

(2) a digit of the foot

(3) writer

(4) storage

(5) sent

(6) screen background

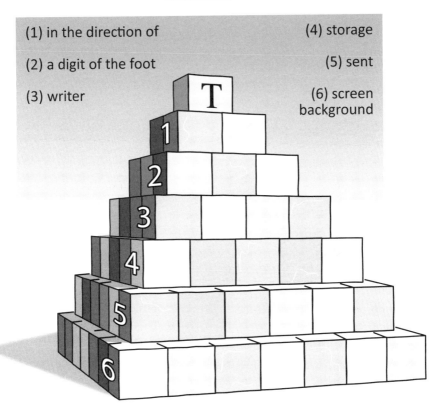

*Each word in the pyramid has the letters of
the word above it, plus a new letter.*

Easy

*What word or concept
is depicted here?*

Easy

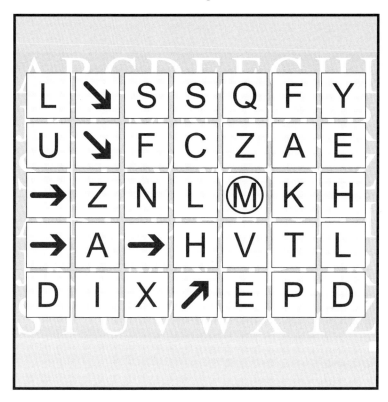

Knowing that every arrow points to a letter and that no letter can touch another vertically, horizontally, or diagonally, find the missing letters that form a key word when read in order. We show one letter in a circle to help you get started.

Medium

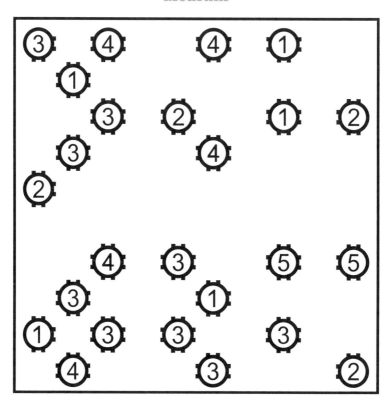

Link all circles with straight horizontal or vertical lines into one connected group. The numbers tell how many lines are connected to a circle. There can be no more than two lines in the same direction and lines cannot cross circles or other lines.

Medium

DATING
GASSES
ICE AGE
IRON
ISLANDS
OCEANS
RIVERS
ROCK
SAVANNAH
SWAMP
TIDES
WATER
WINTER
WOODS
WORLD

K	C	O	R	W	O	O	D	S
E	S	A	V	A	N	N	A	H
W	O	R	L	D	A	O	R	G
A	P	S	R	E	V	I	R	N
T	M	G	A	S	S	E	S	I
E	A	I	C	E	A	G	E	T
R	W	I	N	T	E	R	D	A
I	S	L	A	N	D	S	I	D
O	C	E	A	N	S	T	T	H

*All the words are hidden vertically, horizontally,
or diagonally, in both directions. The letters that remain
unused form a key word when read in order.*

Easy

		5		3				9
					1			4
			8					1
1				6		2		
	7				5	4	9	6
2		9	5		4	6	7	
3	4				8	2		
	1			6		9		8

Fill in the grid so that each row, each column,
and each 3x3 frame contains every number from 1 to 9.

Medium

ACHILLES (2012 Olympic gold medal Swimming Men's 100m Butterfly)

M ☐ ☐ H ☐ E ☐   P ☐ ☐ ☐ P ☐

BASTION (2012 Olympic gold medal Athletics Men's 100m)

U ☐ ☐ ☐ ☐   ☐ ☐ L ☐

Form the word or phrase that is described in parentheses with the letters above the grid. Extra letters are already in the right place.

Hard

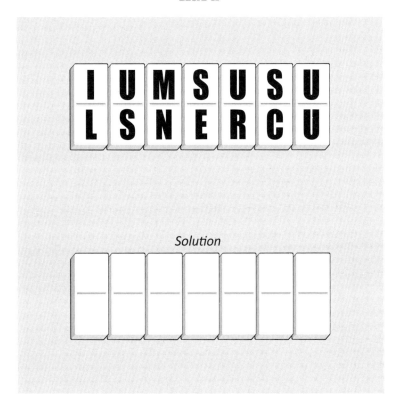

Solution

*Move the letter blocks around to form words on top and below that you can associate with **weather**. The letters are reversed on two blocks.*

Medium

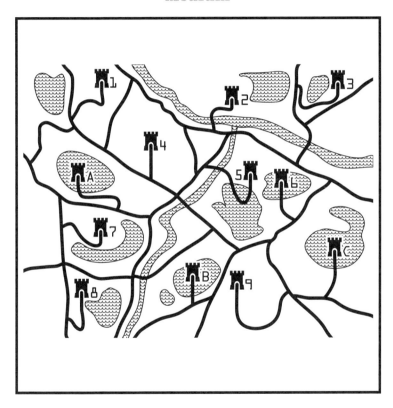

The historian has already visited castles A, B and C.
Which castle (1-9) will he visit next?

Medium

2	2	2	4	1	0
1	3	4	4	3	3
1	3	1		3	5
5	4	2	2	3	3
1	2	1	1	2	2
2	4	1	1	5	5

Draw the shortest path from the ball to the hole. You can only move along vertical and horizontal lines. The figure on each square indicates the number of squares the ball must move in the same direction. You can change direction at each stop.

Hard

*The word below contains the letters of the word
above plus or minus the letter in the middle.
One letter is already in the right place.*

Easy

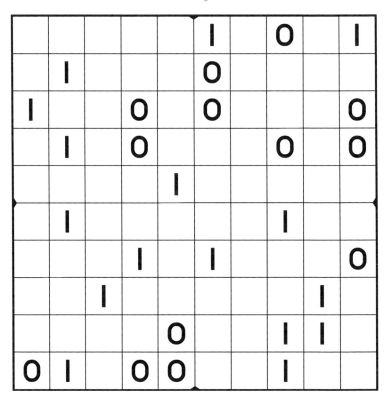

Complete the grid with zeros and ones until there are five zeros and five ones in every row and every column. No more than two of the same number can be next to or under each other. Rows or columns with exactly the same content are not allowed.

Medium

(1) alternative

(2) 2nd largest city of Brazil

(3) public act of violence

(4) proportion

(5) create with cloth

(6) relating to the path of a celestial body

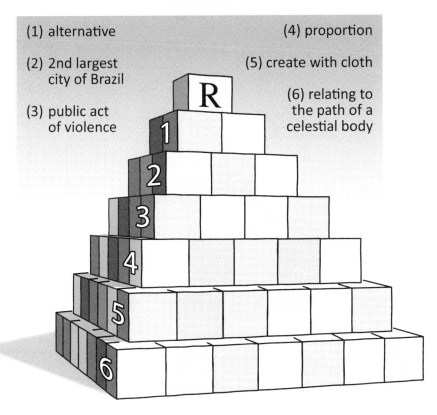

Each word in the pyramid has the letters of the word above it, plus a new letter.

Medium

*What word or concept
is depicted here?*

Medium

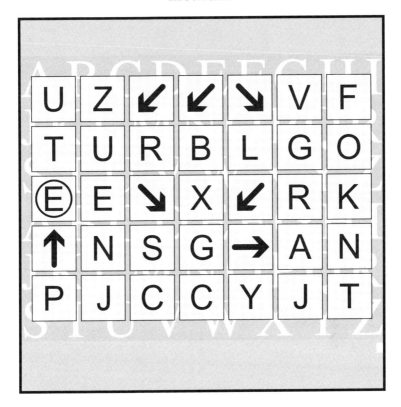

Knowing that every arrow points to a letter and that no letter can touch another vertically, horizontally, or diagonally, find the missing letters that form a key word when read in order. We show one letter in a circle to help you get started.

Hard

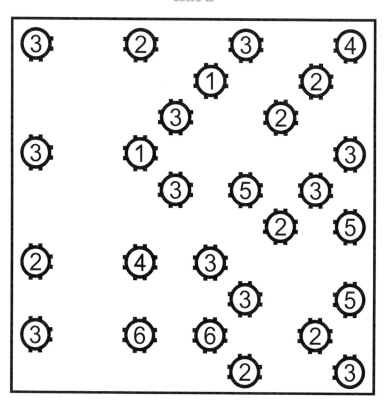

Link all circles with straight horizontal or vertical lines into one connected group. The numbers tell how many lines are connected to a circle. There can be no more than two lines in the same direction and lines cannot cross circles or other lines.

Medium

BLACKJACK
BRIDGE
CLUE
HEARTS
INGENIOUS
MEMORY
POKER
PONTOON
REBUS
RISK
SEESAW
SUDOKU
TAROT
WHIST

S	U	O	I	N	E	G	N	I
C	G	A	T	A	R	O	T	M
M	L	R	E	B	U	S	K	E
E	T	U	K	O	D	U	S	M
G	S	E	E	S	A	W	I	O
D	I	E	P	O	K	E	R	R
I	H	E	A	R	T	S	S	Y
R	W	P	O	N	T	O	O	N
B	L	A	C	K	J	A	C	K

*All the words are hidden vertically, horizontally,
or diagonally, in both directions. The letters that remain
unused form a key word when read in order.*

Medium

7	2	3	5		4			
6	8		2	9	3			5
5	1					2	4	3
				2		4	8	
9			4	3			6	
				6	7			
	3			7				
								8
			1			9		

*Fill in the grid so that each row, each column,
and each 3x3 frame contains every number from 1 to 9.*

Medium

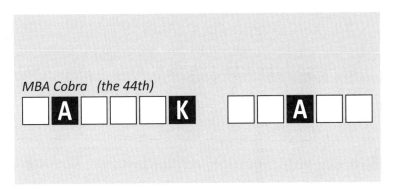

MBA Cobra   (the 44th)

	A				K

		A		

PRINTED (chief)

			S			E		

Form the word or phrase that is described in parentheses with the letters above the grid. Extra letters are already in the right place.

Easy

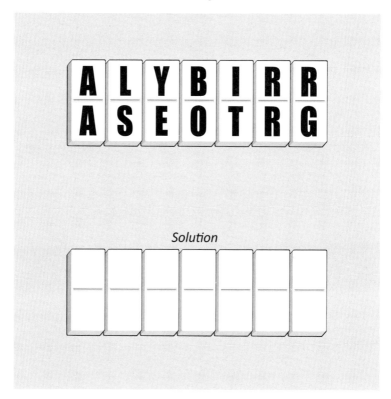

Solution

Move the letter blocks around to form words on top
and below that you can associate with **collections**.

Hard

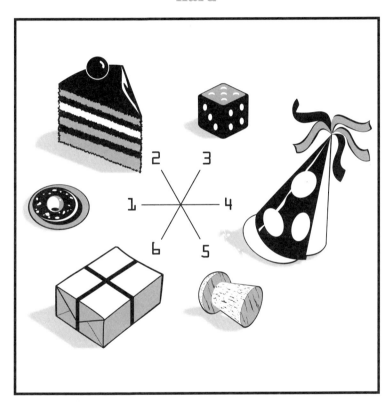

Where (1-6) is the item that is located across from the item that is 3 places anticlockwise from the item that is across from the item to the left of the champagne cork?

Medium

4	3	4	3	5	2
4	3	4	4	2	1
2	3		0	3	4
4	2	3	1	1	5
3	2	4	1	3	1
3	4	4	2	2	3

Draw the shortest path from the ball to the hole. You can only move along vertical and horizontal lines. The figure on each square indicates the number of squares the ball must move in the same direction. You can change direction at each stop.

Hard

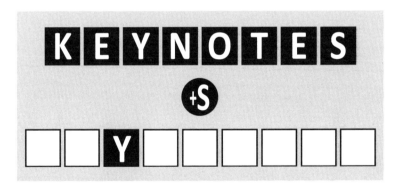

The word below contains the letters of the word above plus or minus the letter in the middle. One letter is already in the right place.

Very Hard

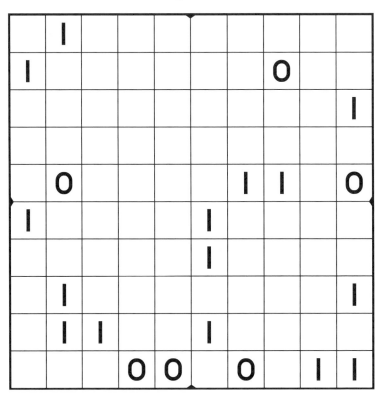

Complete the grid with zeros and ones until there are five zeros and five ones in every row and every column. No more than two of the same number can be next to or under each other. Rows or columns with exactly the same content are not allowed.

Medium

(1) act

(2) couple

(3) loosen

(4) British money

(5) one-legged support

(6) confiscate

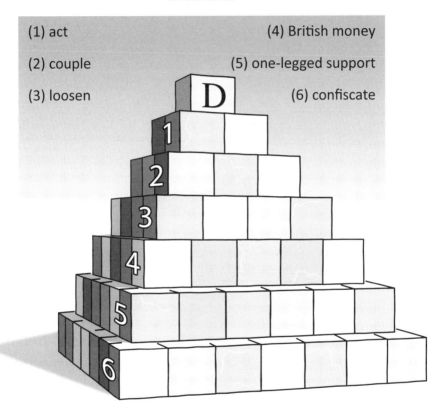

*Each word in the pyramid has the letters of
the word above it, plus a new letter.*

Medium

*What word or concept
is depicted here?*

Hard

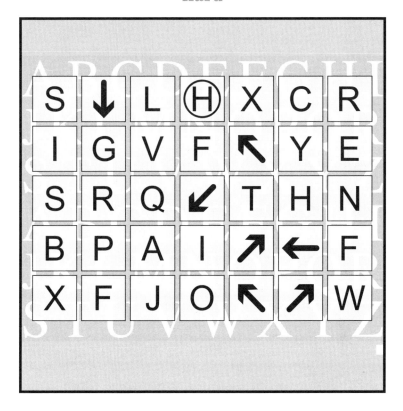

Knowing that every arrow points to a letter and that no letter can touch another vertically, horizontally, or diagonally, find the missing letters that form a key word when read in order. We show one letter in a circle to help you get started.

Easy

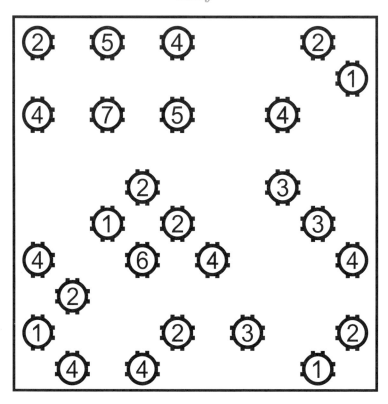

Link all circles with straight horizontal or vertical lines into one connected group. The numbers tell how many lines are connected to a circle. There can be no more than two lines in the same direction and lines cannot cross circles or other lines.

Medium

ALARM
ANDESITE
ARARAT
CRUST
DACITE
DEATH
EIFEL
EMISSION
ETNA
FUJI
JAPAN
KAMCHATKA
LAVA
MAGMA
POMPEII
TOBA

```
A R A R A T V N I
V E O E H M O A I
A I D T T I G P E
L F A I S O L A P
C E C S A T B J M
D L I E N S O A O
S M T D F U J I P
E N E N M R A L A
A K T A H C M A K
```

*All the words are hidden vertically, horizontally,
or diagonally, in both directions. The letters that remain
unused form a key word when read in order.*

Hard

		9						
					4		8	
4	8					3		
	9							8
7	4			5			3	
2		5					1	
		1			8	6		2
			3	4	6		7	1
				1			5	

Fill in the grid so that each row, each column,
and each 3x3 frame contains every number from 1 to 9.

Medium

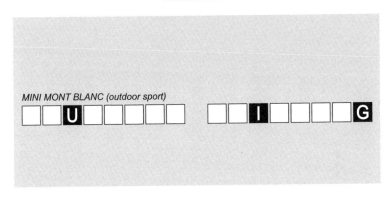

MINI MONT BLANC (outdoor sport)

WEST GIRL (hand-to-hand combat)

Form the word or phrase that is described in parentheses with the letters above the grid. Extra letters are already in the right place.

Medium

Solution

Move the letter blocks around to form words on top
and below that you can associate with **insects**.
The letters are reversed on one block.

Medium

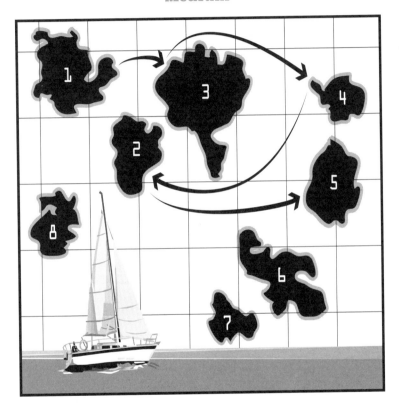

*In which order will the yacht visit
the three remaining islands?*

Medium

3	5	5	2	1	1
1	2	4	4	1	5
5		3	3	3	3
1	4	3	1	4	1
5	3	2	2	1	2
3	1	3	1	1	3

Draw the shortest path from the ball to the hole. You can only move along vertical and horizontal lines. The figure on each square indicates the number of squares the ball must move in the same direction. You can change direction at each stop.

Hard

*The word below contains the letters of the word
above plus or minus the letter in the middle.
One letter is already in the right place.*

Medium

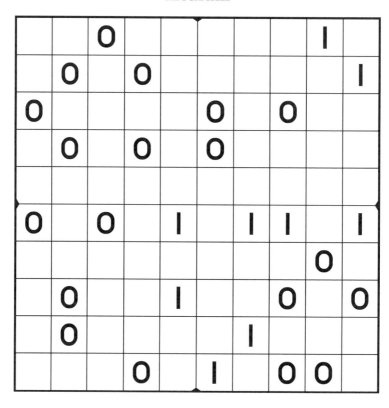

Complete the grid with zeros and ones until there are five zeros and five ones in every row and every column. No more than two of the same number can be next to or under each other. Rows or columns with exactly the same content are not allowed.

Medium

(1) mother

(2) heading

(3) female domestic

(4) means of mass communication

(5) look up to

(6) half fish

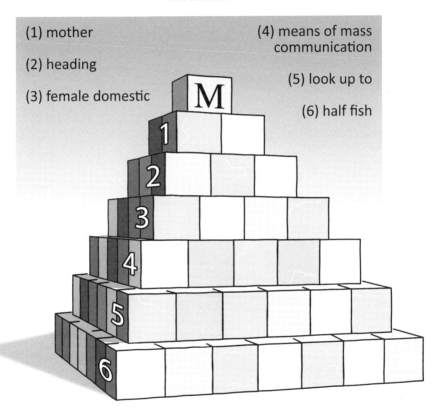

Each word in the pyramid has the letters of the word above it, plus a new letter.

Hard

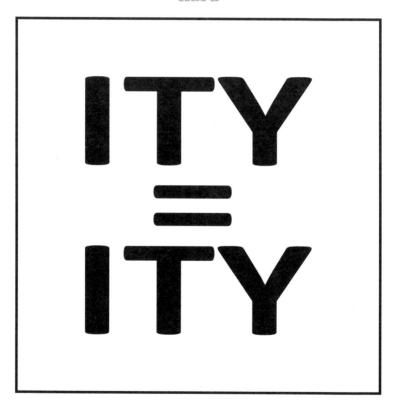

*What word or concept
is depicted here?*

Easy

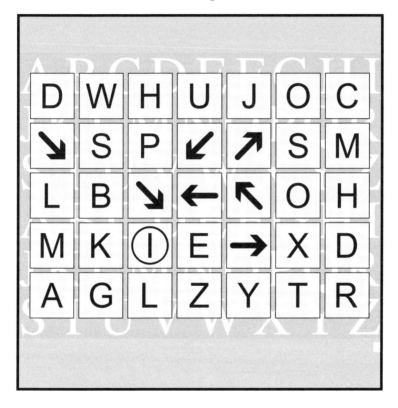

Knowing that every arrow points to a letter and that no letter can touch another vertically, horizontally, or diagonally, find the missing letters that form a key word when read in order. We show one letter in a circle to help you get started.

Very Hard

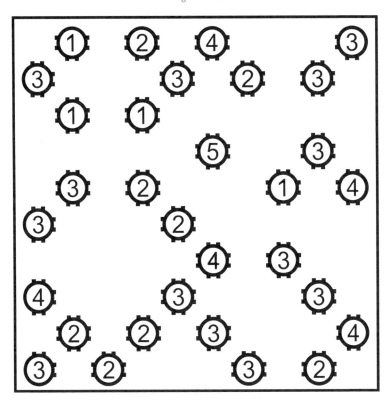

Link all circles with straight horizontal or vertical lines into
one connected group. The numbers tell how many lines are
connected to a circle. There can be no more than two lines in
the same direction and lines cannot cross circles or other lines.

If you can't solve certain puzzles, don't look up the answers — just try again later.

Finding the solution is much more fun than knowing the solution.

page 7
SLEEP

page 8

7	6	9	3	8	5	1	2	4
2	4	5	7	1	6	8	9	3
3	8	1	9	4	2	7	5	6
6	5	2	4	7	1	3	8	9
9	7	3	5	6	8	4	1	2
8	1	4	2	9	3	6	7	5
1	2	8	6	5	4	9	3	7
5	9	6	1	3	7	2	4	8
4	3	7	8	2	9	5	6	1

page 9
- GEORGE LAZENBY
- FROM RUSSIA
  WITH LOVE

page 10
TEACHER
DENTIST

page 11
N. All letters that only appear once have a white outline.

page 12

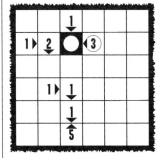

page 13
AFFLICT
STREAMING

page 14

I	O	I	I	O	O	I	O	I	O
O	I	O	I	O	I	O	I	I	O
I	O	I	O	I	O	O	I	O	I
O	I	O	O	I	O	I	O	I	I
O	O	I	I	O	I	O	I	I	O
I	O	O	I	I	O	I	O	O	I
O	I	I	O	O	I	O	I	O	I
I	O	O	I	O	I	I	O	I	O
I	I	O	O	I	O	I	O	O	I
O	I	I	O	I	I	O	I	O	O

page 15
(1) AM
(2) BAM
(3) BEAM
(4) BLAME
(5) MARBLE
(6) RAMBLER

page 16
AIRBAG

page 17
ADMIRAL

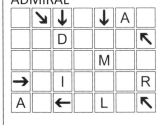

page 18

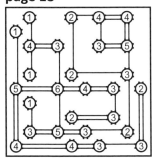

page 19
AIRPLANE

page 20

1	2	3	7	5	9	6	8	4
6	4	9	1	8	3	7	5	2
5	7	8	4	6	2	3	1	9
8	5	1	2	4	6	9	3	7
4	9	7	3	1	5	2	6	8
3	6	2	8	9	7	1	4	5
2	3	4	6	7	8	5	9	1
7	1	5	9	3	4	8	2	6
9	8	6	5	2	1	4	7	3

page 21
BASKETBALL
LACROSSE

page 22
BROTHER
HUSBAND

page 23
9. The rooms located one floor higher use the average of the two rooms below.

page 24

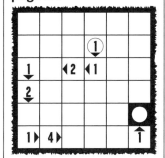

page 25
FRAGILE
MISPLACED

page 26

0	0	I	I	0	I	0	0	I	I
0	0	I	I	0	I	0	I	0	I
I	I	0	0	I	0	I	I	0	0
I	I	0	0	I	I	0	0	I	0
0	0	I	I	0	I	I	0	0	I
I	I	0	I	I	0	0	I	0	0
0	0	I	0	I	0	I	0	I	I
I	0	I	0	0	I	0	I	I	0
0	I	0	I	0	0	I	I	0	I
I	I	0	0	I	0	I	0	I	0

page 27
(1) IN
(2) ION
(3) COIN
(4) TONIC
(5) ACTION
(6) CAUTION

page 28
Shake R = SHAKER

page 29
TESTING

page 30

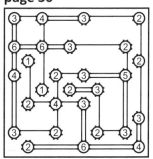

page 31

THRILLER

page 32

4	3	6	5	1	2	7	8	9
7	5	1	4	8	9	3	6	2
2	8	9	6	7	3	1	4	5
5	1	3	7	4	6	2	9	8
8	9	7	2	5	1	4	3	6
6	4	2	3	9	8	5	1	7
1	2	4	8	6	5	9	7	3
9	6	5	1	3	7	8	2	4
3	7	8	9	2	4	6	5	1

page 33

ASTRONOMER
STREET MAP

page 34

LINCOLN
MERCURY

page 35

9. The sum of the points on two cans in the back row is equal to the number of points on the can in front of them. So 4+2= 6, 2+7= 9, etc.

page 36

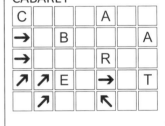

page 37

BOREDOM
MECHANICS

page 38

0	I	I	0	0	I	I	0	0	I
I	0	I	0	0	I	0	I	0	I
0	I	0	I	I	0	0	I	I	0
I	0	0	I	0	I	I	0	0	I
0	0	I	0	I	I	0	I	I	0
0	I	0	0	I	0	I	0	I	I
I	I	0	I	0	0	I	I	0	0
I	0	I	I	0	I	0	0	I	0
0	0	I	0	I	0	I	0	I	I
I	I	0	I	I	0	0	I	0	0

page 39

(1) GO
(2) EGO
(3) GORE
(4) ROUGE
(5) MORGUE
(6) GOURMET

page 40

CATWALK

page 41

CABARET

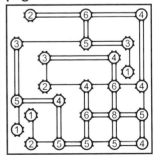

page 42

page 43

CHESS

page 44

3	4	1	7	9	6	8	2	5
2	8	6	3	4	5	1	7	9
7	9	5	2	1	8	6	4	3
1	7	2	6	3	4	9	5	8
5	3	9	8	7	2	4	6	1
4	6	8	9	5	1	7	3	2
6	2	3	4	8	9	5	1	7
8	1	7	5	6	3	2	9	4
9	5	4	1	2	7	3	8	6

page 45

SNOWBOARDING
BUNGEE JUMP

page 46

PROCESS
SUSPECT

page 47

Mary. The two names of each couple contain the same vowels.

page 48

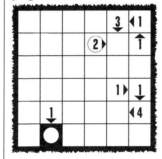

page 49

CLEANED
TRANSPIRE

page 50

O	I	O	I	I	O	O	I	I	O
O	O	I	I	O	I	O	I	I	O
I	O	I	O	O	I	I	O	O	I
I	I	O	O	I	O	O	I	O	I
O	O	I	I	O	I	I	O	I	O
I	I	O	O	I	O	I	O	I	O
O	O	I	O	I	I	O	I	O	I
I	I	O	I	O	I	O	O	I	O
I	I	O	O	I	O	I	O	O	I
O	O	I	I	O	O	I	I	O	I

page 51

(1) ME
(2) REM
(3) MORE
(4) METRO
(5) MOTHER
(6) THERMOS

page 52

FACEBOOK

page 53

CREATOR

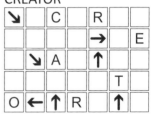

page 54

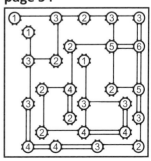

page 55
JAZZ

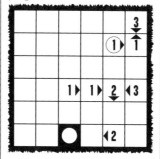

Word search grid:
```
R A B B E B O P J
E B A A B L U E S
I U K V O O D O O
N T E S E V A L S
H T R U M P E T E
A K P I A N O Z L
R N A C I R F A I
D O Z E V A N S M
T M I M P U L S E
```

page 56
```
8 6 9 3 1 5 2 7 4
3 1 2 8 7 4 5 6 9
7 5 4 2 6 9 8 3 1
6 4 5 9 3 8 7 1 2
1 7 3 4 2 6 9 5 8
2 9 8 7 5 1 3 4 6
5 2 6 1 8 7 4 9 3
9 3 7 6 4 2 1 8 5
4 8 1 5 9 3 6 2 7
```

page 57
NEBRASKA
NEW MEXICO

page 58
SIXTEEN
SEVENTY

page 59
Group 2. In all the other groups, the shape of the white chocolate on the biscuit refers to the shape of the other biscuit.

page 60

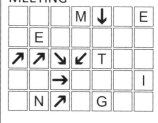

page 61
ONBOARD
CASSEROLE

page 62
0	I	0	I	0	I	0	I	0
I	0	I	0	I	0	I	0	I
I	I	0	0	I	0	I	I	0
0	0	I	I	0	I	0	I	0
I	0	I	I	0	0	I	0	I
0	I	0	0	I	I	0	0	I
I	I	0	0	I	0	0	I	0
0	0	I	I	0	I	I	0	I
0	0	I	0	I	I	0	I	I
I	I	0	I	0	0	I	I	0

page 63
(1) AN
(2) ANT
(3) NATO
(4) TANGO
(5) NOUGAT
(6) HANGOUT

page 64
COFFEE BREAK

page 65
MEETING

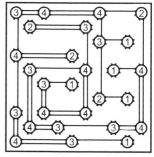

page 66

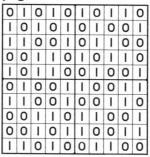

page 67
ALPINISM

page 68

9	1	2	6	5	3	7	4	8
4	5	7	8	1	2	9	6	3
6	8	3	7	9	4	2	1	5
7	3	6	5	2	1	8	9	4
2	4	8	3	6	9	5	7	1
1	9	5	4	7	8	3	2	6
5	6	4	2	3	7	1	8	9
8	7	1	9	4	5	6	3	2
3	2	9	1	8	6	4	5	7

page 69
COLLEGE TUITION
FINANCIAL CRISIS

page 70
HURDLES
JAVELIN

page 71
11. Read as follows:
41-17-14=10,
37-21-5= 11.

page 72

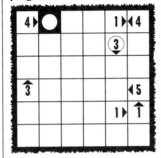

page 73
PARROTS
LISTENING

page 74

0	I	0	I	0	0	I	0	I	I
I	0	0	I	I	0	I	0	0	I
I	0	I	0	0	I	0	I	I	0
0	I	I	0	I	I	0	I	0	0
0	I	0	I	I	0	I	0	0	I
I	0	I	0	0	I	I	0	I	0
0	I	0	I	I	0	0	I	I	0
0	I	I	0	I	0	I	0	0	I
I	0	0	I	0	I	0	I	I	0
I	0	I	0	0	I	0	I	0	I

page 75
(1) AT
(2) TAP
(3) TAPE
(4) ADEPT
(5) DEPART
(6) TRAPPED

page 76
MIS under STAND in G
= MISUNDERSTANDING

page 77
OCTOBER

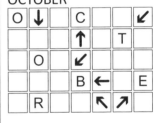

page 78

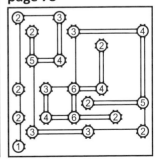

page 79
RIVERS

page 80

2	5	7	4	8	3	6	9	1
3	1	6	9	7	2	8	4	5
9	4	8	1	6	5	3	7	2
8	6	3	7	2	9	1	5	4
5	2	1	8	4	6	7	3	9
4	7	9	5	3	1	2	6	8
6	9	5	2	1	7	4	8	3
1	3	4	6	5	8	9	2	7
7	8	2	3	9	4	5	1	6

page 81
DERMATOLOGIST
ORNITHOLOGIST

page 82
CHOPPER
SCOOTER

page 83
Flower branch 2.
The top flower of all
the other branches has
just as many petals as
flowers on the branch.

page 84

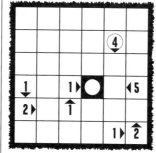

page 85
WARHEAD
CORPORATE

page 86

0	0	I	0	I	I	0	I	I	0
0	0	I	I	0	0	I	0	I	I
I	I	0	0	I	0	0	I	0	I
0	I	0	I	0	I	0	I	I	0
I	0	I	0	0	I	I	0	I	0
I	0	0	I	I	0	I	0	0	I
0	I	0	0	I	I	0	I	0	I
I	0	I	I	0	0	I	0	I	0
I	I	0	I	0	I	0	I	0	0
0	I	I	0	I	0	I	0	0	I

page 87
(1) BE
(2) BEE
(3) BEER
(4) REBEL
(5) TREBLE
(6) TREMBLE

page 88
Thin king = THINKING

page 89
EXPLORE

page 90

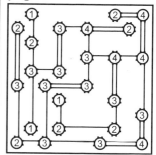

page 91
FRUIT

page 92

3	2	4	5	6	7	1	9	8
8	1	6	3	9	2	5	4	7
7	5	9	4	1	8	3	6	2
2	7	3	9	8	1	4	5	6
4	6	5	2	7	3	8	1	9
9	8	1	6	5	4	2	7	3
1	4	7	8	3	6	9	2	5
5	3	2	7	4	9	6	8	1
6	9	8	1	2	5	7	3	4

page 93
CALIFORNIA CONDOR
AFRICAN ELEPHANT

page 94
TEMPLE
TONGUE

page 95
Sthoma. Starting with Thomas the letters rotate from front to back. Thomas, Homast, Omasth, Mastho, Asthom and Sthoma.

page 96

2▶	5	◀1			
				2	
↑2			◀4		
			↑1		
1▶	○				

page 97
MASTERS
INTRODUCE

page 98

0	I	I	0	I	0	0	I	0	I
I	0	I	0	0	I	0	I	I	0
0	I	0	I	0	I	I	0	I	0
I	0	0	I	I	0	I	0	0	I
0	I	I	0	I	I	0	I	0	0
I	0	0	I	0	I	I	0	I	0
0	I	I	0	I	0	I	0	0	I
0	0	I	I	0	I	0	I	I	0
I	0	0	I	0	0	I	0	I	I
I	I	0	0	I	0	0	I	0	I

page 99
(1) HE
(2) HER
(3) HARE
(4) EARTH
(5) THREAT
(6) THEATER

page 100
AR two RK = ARTWORK

page 101
VANILLA

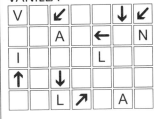

page 102

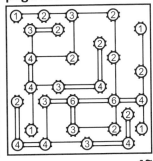

page 103
OPERA

page 104

9	1	4	3	7	5	2	6	8
2	7	6	9	1	8	5	4	3
5	8	3	2	6	4	9	7	1
7	9	8	6	4	3	1	2	5
6	2	5	8	9	1	4	3	7
4	3	1	5	2	7	8	9	6
8	6	7	4	5	9	3	1	2
1	5	9	7	3	2	6	8	4
3	4	2	1	8	6	7	5	9

page 105
DEMOCRATIC
REPUBLICAN

page 106
BOLERO
FOXTROT

page 107
Butterfly D. The right top wing and the left bottom wing is the same color as the outer edge of the wings of all the other butterflies. D is different.

page 108

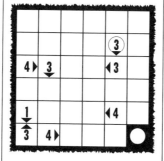

page 109
ORPHANS
ANTITRUST

page 110

I	0	I	0	I	0	I	0	I	0
0	I	0	I	0	I	0	I	I	0
0	0	I	I	0	I	0	I	0	I
I	I	0	0	I	0	I	0	0	I
0	I	I	0	0	I	0	I	I	0
I	0	0	I	0	0	I	0	I	I
I	I	0	0	I	I	0	I	0	0
0	0	I	I	0	I	I	0	0	I
0	0	I	0	I	0	I	0	I	I
I	I	0	I	I	0	0	I	0	0

page 111
(1) NO
(2) EON
(3) NOSE
(4) NOISE
(5) SENIOR
(6) VERSION

page 112
CIN east = CINEAST

page 113
QUARREL

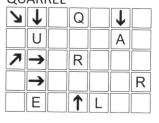

page 114

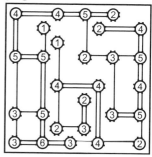

page 115

BODY

page 116

7	6	9	3	1	8	5	2	4
5	4	3	2	7	9	1	6	8
8	1	2	5	4	6	9	7	3
9	3	8	6	5	1	2	4	7
2	7	6	9	3	4	8	5	1
1	5	4	8	2	7	3	9	6
3	9	7	1	6	5	4	8	2
4	2	5	7	8	3	6	1	9
6	8	1	4	9	2	7	3	5

page 117

WEATHER FRONT
THUNDERSTORM

page 118

DESPAIR
PASSION

page 119

Six of hearts. The same cards are used in every column.

page 120

page 121

PIGEONS
DISAPPEAR

page 122

0	0	1	1	0	1	1	0	0	1
1	0	0	1	0	1	0	1	0	1
0	1	1	0	1	0	0	1	1	0
0	1	0	0	1	0	1	0	1	1
1	0	1	1	0	1	0	1	0	0
1	1	0	0	1	1	0	0	1	0
0	1	0	0	1	0	1	1	0	1
0	0	1	1	0	0	1	1	0	1
1	0	1	0	1	1	0	0	1	0
1	1	0	1	0	0	1	0	1	0

page 123

(1) TO
(2) TOE
(3) POET
(4) DEPOT
(5) POSTED
(6) DESKTOP

page 124

WALLSTREET

page 125

FEMALE

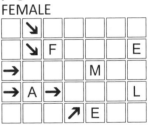

page 126

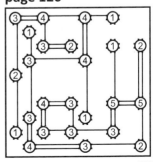

page 127

EARTH

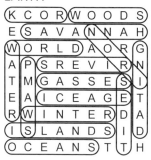

page 128

7	3	1	8	4	9	5	6	2
4	6	5	7	3	2	1	8	9
9	2	8	6	5	1	7	3	4
6	9	2	4	8	7	3	5	1
1	5	4	3	9	6	8	2	7
8	7	3	1	2	5	4	9	6
2	8	9	5	1	4	6	7	3
3	4	6	9	7	8	2	1	5
5	1	7	2	6	3	9	4	8

page 129

MICHAEL PHELPS
USAIN BOLT

page 130

CUMULUS
SUNRISE

page 131

Castle 6. The historian is only interested in water fortresses.

page 132

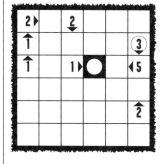

page 133

ARSENIC
HARMONICA

page 134

I	0	0	I	0	I	I	0	0	I
0	I	0	I	I	0	I	0	0	I
I	0	I	0	I	0	0	I	I	0
0	I	I	0	0	I	I	0	I	0
I	0	0	I	I	0	I	0	0	I
0	I	I	0	I	0	0	I	I	0
I	I	0	I	0	I	0	I	0	0
0	0	I	0	I	0	I	0	I	I
I	0	0	I	0	I	0	I	I	0
0	I	I	0	0	I	0	I	0	I

page 135

(1) OR
(2) RIO
(3) RIOT
(4) RATIO
(5) TAILOR
(6) ORBITAL

page 136

HEADHUNTER

page 137

URGENCY

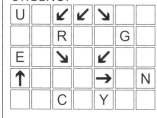

page 138

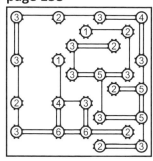

page 139
GAMES

page 140

7	2	3	5	1	4	8	9	6
6	8	4	2	9	3	1	7	5
5	1	9	7	8	6	2	4	3
3	7	6	9	2	5	4	8	1
9	5	8	4	3	1	7	6	2
1	4	2	8	6	7	3	5	9
8	3	1	6	7	9	5	2	4
4	9	7	3	5	2	6	1	8
2	6	5	1	4	8	9	3	7

page 141
BARACK OBAMA
PRESIDENT

page 142
LIBRARY
STORAGE

page 143
Dice on 3.

page 144

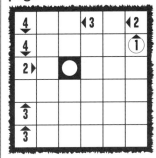

page 145
LEASING
KEYSTONES

page 146

0	1	0	1	1	0	0	1	1	0
1	0	0	1	1	0	1	0	1	0
0	1	1	0	0	1	0	1	0	1
0	0	1	1	0	0	1	0	1	1
1	0	0	1	1	0	1	1	0	0
1	1	0	0	1	1	0	1	0	0
0	0	1	0	0	1	1	0	1	1
1	1	0	1	0	0	1	0	0	1
0	1	1	0	1	1	0	1	0	0
1	0	1	0	0	1	0	0	1	1

page 147
(1) DO
(2) DUO
(3) UNDO
(4) POUND
(5) UNIPOD
(6) IMPOUND

page 148
GR ape = GRAPE

page 149
SHERIFF

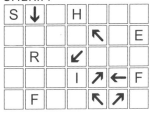

page 150

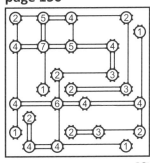

page 151
VOLCANOS

page 152

3	1	9	7	8	5	4	2	6
5	2	6	9	3	4	1	8	7
4	8	7	1	6	2	3	9	5
1	9	3	4	2	7	5	6	8
7	4	8	6	5	1	2	3	9
2	6	5	8	9	3	7	1	4
9	3	1	5	7	8	6	4	2
8	5	2	3	4	6	9	7	1
6	7	4	2	1	9	8	5	3

page 153
MOUNTAIN CLIMBING
WRESTLING

page 154
SPIDER
CRICKET

page 155
8-6-7.
The yacht always sails
to the next island that
is a bit farther south.

page 156

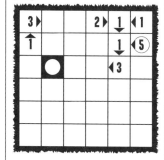

page 157
MONARCH
OFFICINAL

page 158

0	I	0	I	0	I	0	I	I	0
I	0	I	0	0	I	0	0	I	I
0	I	0	I	I	0	I	0	0	I
I	0	I	0	I	0	0	I	I	0
I	0	I	I	0	I	0	0	I	0
0	I	0	0	I	0	I	I	0	I
0	I	0	I	0	0	I	I	0	I
I	0	I	0	I	I	0	0	I	0
I	0	0	I	I	0	I	I	0	0
0	I	I	0	0	I	I	0	0	I

page 159
(1) MA
(2) AIM
(3) MAID
(4) MEDIA
(5) ADMIRE
(6) MERMAID

page 160
equal ITY = EQUALITY

page 161
HOLIDAY

page 162

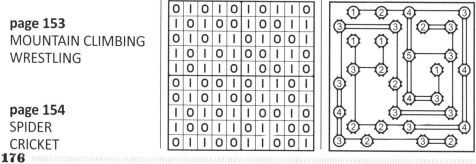